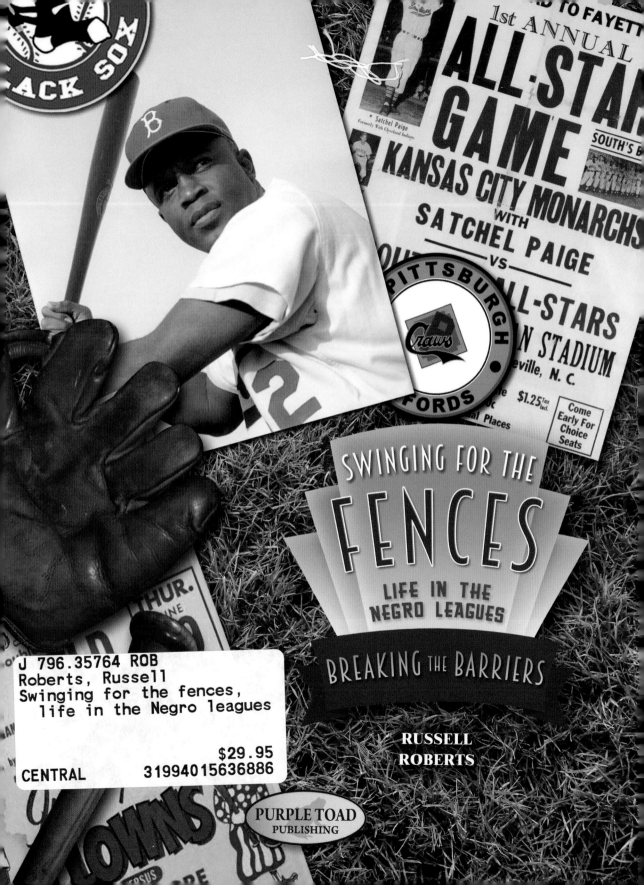

SWINGING FOR THE

FENCES

LIFE IN THE NEGRO LEAGUES

BREAKING THE BARRIERS

**RUSSELL
ROBERTS**

PURPLE TOAD
PUBLISHING

Printing   1   2   3   4   5   6   7   8   9

PUBLISHER'S NOTE
This series, Swinging for the Fences: Life in the Negro Leagues, covers racism in United States history and how it affected professional baseball. Some of the events told in this series may be disturbing to young readers.

SWINGING FOR THE
FENCES
LIFE IN THE
NEGRO LEAGUES

A 4 VOL. SERIES

A Whole New League
by Wayne L. Wilson
Barnstorming
by Michael DeMocker
Legends of the Leagues
by Pete DiPrimio
Breaking the Barriers
by Russell Roberts

ABOUT THE AUTHOR: Russell Roberts has researched, written, and published numerous books for both children and adults. Among his books for adults are *Down the Jersey Shore, Historical Photos of New Jersey,* and *Ten Days to a Sharper Memory.* He has written over 50 nonfiction books for children. Roberts often speaks on the subjects of his books before various groups and organizations. He lives in New Jersey.

Publisher's Cataloging-in-Publication Data
Roberts, Russell.
   Breaking the barriers / written by Russell Roberts.
     p. cm.
Includes bibliographic references, glossary, and index.
ISBN 9781624692840
1. Negro leagues—History—Juvenile literature. 2. Baseball—United States—History—Juvenile literature. I. Series: Swinging For The Fences : Life in the Negro Leagues.
  GV865.A1 2017
  796.357
Library of Congress Control Number: 2016937176
ebook ISBN: 9781624692857

TICKETS

"MY SKIN IS AGAINST ME"

CHAPTER ONE

The ban against African-American players in professional baseball began in a time of hope.

By 1867, slavery was over in the United States. Black people in America were confident that their lives would be different now. The future shone with promise.

In December of that year, however, that promise was starting to fade. The nominating committee of the National Association of Base Ball Players (NABBP) held a meeting in Philadelphia. The members were white team owners. They voted to ban "any club which may be composed of one or more colored persons."[1] The NABBP governed baseball. This group made the rules for the league.

There was never a specific written rule barring blacks in organized baseball. It was simply understood by all club owners that no one would allow a black player on their team. It was called a

U.S. President Abraham Lincoln signed the Emancipation Proclamation, ending slavery in the United States in 1863. African-Americans saw that freedom and equality could finally be theirs. In reality, the end of slavery was just the first step.

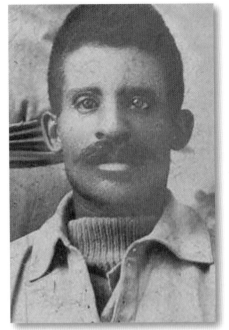

Gentlemen's Agreement. No one dared violate it and get the other owners angry.

The NABBP's action did not immediately bar black players from organized baseball. Black and white players still played side by side during the 1870s and 1880s. However, black players became fewer and fewer as the ban spread, and new contracts were not signed.

One victim of the ban was Bud Fowler. Fowler was an excellent second baseman. He is often considered the first black professional baseball player (meaning that he was paid to play). However, he

Bud Fowler

only played in the minors. The Gentlemen's Agreement kept him from ever moving up to the major leagues. "My skin is against me. If I had not been quite so black," he said, "I might have caught on as a Spaniard or something."[2]

In 1884, catcher Moses Fleetwood Walker became the first black player in the major leagues. The Toledo club he played for joined the major league American Association. Unfortunately, bigotry dogged Walker like a curse. Pitcher Tony

Oberlin College 1881 baseball team, with Fleetwood Walker (middle, left) and his brother, Weldy (No. 10)

Mullane, for example, refused to take Walker's signals. "I had it in for him," Mullane remembered. "He was the best catcher I ever worked with, but I disliked a Negro catcher."[3]

Catchers wore no protective equipment at the time. With his pitcher working against him, Walker never knew what pitch was coming. He was often injured.

A famous racial incident concerning Walker involved Adrian "Cap" Anson. Anson was a superstar in baseball's early days—but he did not want to play with blacks. One day Anson's Chicago White Stockings were going to play Toledo. When Anson saw Walker, he threatened to pull his team off the field. Anson finally played only because he was told he would not get paid if he didn't play.

Moses Fleetwood Walker (top row, middle) was a catcher for Toledo.

Cap Anson

In 1887, three things happened to further push blacks out of baseball. First, nearly every member of the St. Louis Browns signed a petition, saying they refused to play with black men. It was, they said, the right thing to do. The second involved Cap Anson. He learned that a black pitcher named George Stovey was about to join the New York Giants. Anson said that neither he nor his team would ever play the Giants. This time his threat made waves. Stovey was not signed. The third was an order to the secretary of the International League. He was not allowed to approve any more contracts with black players.

By 1901 there was excitement in America. There was an energetic young president in the White House named Theodore Roosevelt. The country was modernizing: Automobiles were replacing horses. Motion pictures were starting to catch on. The telephone instantly connected people across the miles.

New rules were modernizing baseball too. Foul bunts were now called strikes. A held foul tip was a strike. The infield fly rule had been adopted. Catchers were required to stay behind the batter.

However, for African-Americans in baseball, there was no excitement. For them, the Gentlemen's Agreement had slammed baseball's door shut like a heavy iron gate. It would remain tightly closed for decades to come.

John McGraw and Charlie Grant

John McGraw

Occasionally someone tried to get around the Gentlemen's Agreement. In 1901 Baltimore manager John McGraw tried to add African-American second baseman Charlie Grant to his roster. He claimed Grant was really a Cherokee Indian named Charlie Tokahoma. The deception was soon discovered, and Grant never played for Baltimore.

Charlie Grant (right) was fast and quick (one of his nicknames was Speedy). He might well have made a name for himself in professional baseball, but the color line prevented him from signing.

On December 17, 1903, something amazing happened on the wind-swept sand dunes of Kitty Hawk, North Carolina. Two bicycle shop owners from Ohio made the world's first manned flight in a heavier-than-air machine. Their names were Orville and Wilbur Wright.

Professional baseball also had a milestone year. On October 1, the first World Series game was played. It pitted the Boston Pilgrims (Red Sox) against the Pittsburg Pirates. (The Pilgrims won the best-of-nine series, five games to three.)

And in Indiana, another important incident took place. Branch Rickey lost his patience.

Branch Rickey was a coach and catcher for the Ohio Wesleyan baseball team. The team was in

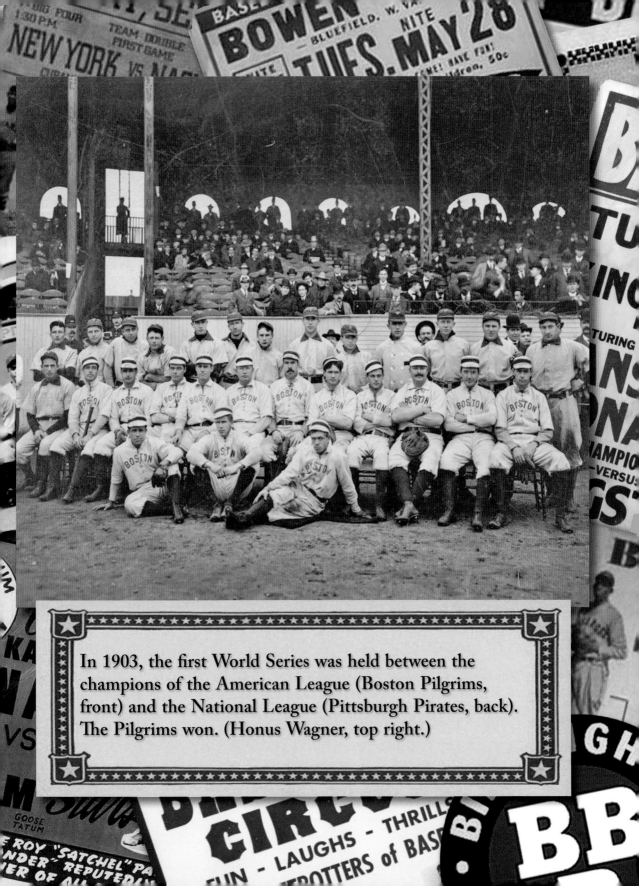

In 1903, the first World Series was held between the champions of the American League (Boston Pilgrims, front) and the National League (Pittsburgh Pirates, back). The Pilgrims won. (Honus Wagner, top right.)

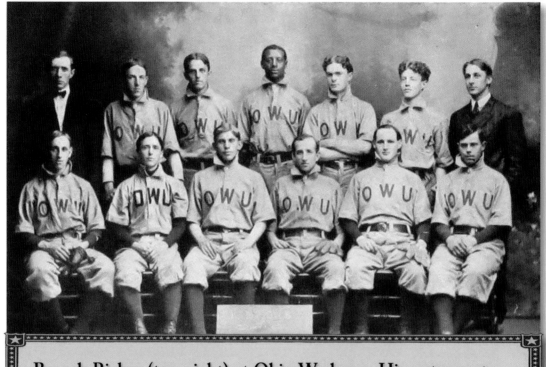

Branch Rickey (top, right) at Ohio Wesleyan. His outrage at the racist treatment of teammate Charles Thomas (top, middle) provided the spark that would one day end baseball's color line.

South Bend, Indiana, for an away game. The manager of the Oliver Hotel told Rickey that his teammate Charles Thomas could not stay at the hotel. "We don't let in nigras," said the manager.[1]

Furious, Rickey dragged a cot into his own room. He thundered that Thomas could stay with him. The manager gave in and let him stay, but he warned Rickey that Thomas could not go anywhere else in the hotel, especially the dining room.

Once in Rickey's room, tears filled Thomas' eyes. "Black skin," he said sadly, rubbing his large hands together as if to wipe away a stain. "If only I could make my black skin white."[2]

Rickey never forgot that sad scene.

Wesley Branch Rickey was born on December 20, 1881, in Stockdale, Ohio. He began his front-office career in baseball with the St. Louis Browns in 1913. In 1919 he moved to the cross-town St. Louis Cardinals. There he developed new ideas, including the farm system, which all major league teams would one day use. In 1942, Rickey was hired by the Brooklyn Dodgers to be president and general manager.

Ever since the early 1900s, Brooklyn fans had been watching good black baseball teams like the Royal Giants.

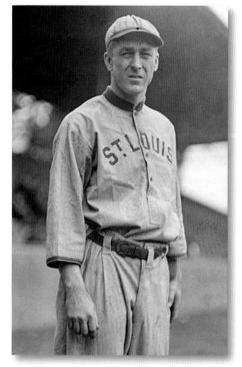

Rickey with the Cardinals

They saw black greats, such as Bruce Petway, Louis Santop, and "Cannonball" Dick Redding. Brooklyn people were hardworking. The population was a mixture of races and nationalities.

When Rickey moved to the Brooklyn Dodgers, he felt it was the perfect place to break the baseball color line. He said he wanted "to do something about Negro participation in baseball."[3]

Rickey was no different than other general managers when it came to player contracts. He was a shrewd

Rickey with the Dodgers

At Brooklyn's Plymouth Church, attendees would sometimes be surprised with a guest sermon delivered by Branch Rickey.

negotiator. He was also an innovator. In addition to creating the farm system, he used sandpits to teach players how to slide and even hired a statistics analyst. All are common practice today. He also believed that baseball set the tone for America. "Baseball should lead by example,"[4] he said. It upset him that bigotry existed both in the game and in the country as a whole.

Religion played a major part in Rickey's decision to sign Jackie Robinson. One day early in 1945, Rickey visited his friend the Reverend Dr. L. Wendell Fifield at Brooklyn's Plymouth Church. Saying nothing, Rickey paced around the office for nearly an hour, lost in thought.

Finally he said, "Wendell, I've decided to sign Jackie Robinson. I had to talk to God about it and be sure what He wanted me to do."[5]

The player Rickey was referring to was Jack Roosevelt Robinson. He was born on January 31, 1919, in Cairo, Georgia. His family moved to Pasadena, California, when he was a small child. There, the Robinsons faced open racism. Their neighbors even tried to have them evicted from their home.

Jackie went to Pasadena Junior College, where he became a four-sport standout (baseball, football, basketball, and track). In 1939 he entered UCLA (University of California, Los Angeles).

Jackie Robinson on the UCLA track team

Boxing champion Joe Louis protested the lack of black officers at Fort Riley and helped Robinson become a second lieutenant in 1943.

There he was called "Lightning Jack" because of his sports skills.

In the spring of 1942, he was drafted into the army. He found that racism existed there, too. In July 1944, he was told to move to the back of a bus (the front was reserved for white riders). He refused and was court-martialed. He was found not guilty and received an honorable discharge from the army in November 1944.

Shortly thereafter he joined the Kansas City Monarchs, one of the Negro League's top teams. Playing shortstop, he hit .345 for the Monarchs. He was quick and daring on the bases.

Meanwhile, Rickey was searching for the player he felt would be right to break baseball's color line. He rejected big-name stars Josh Gibson and Satchel Paige. Rickey didn't think that they could handle the intense media and public pressure that the first black ballplayer to break the color line would face. He also wanted the player to be a World War II veteran. This would help people accept him, Rickey thought. After considering many players, Rickey chose Robinson.

Robinson played in the Negro League All-Star Game in his first year with Kansas City.

Rickey brought Robinson to his Brooklyn office on August 28, 1945. For three hours he lectured, preached, urged, begged, and insulted the young man. He tried to communicate the wide range of experiences that Robinson would face as the first African-American in professional baseball in decades.

At one point, Robinson said, "Mr. Rickey, do you want a Negro who's afraid to fight back?"[6]

Rickey answered, "I'm looking for someone who has the courage not to fight back. You are carrying the reputation of a race on your shoulders. Bear it well and a day will come when every team in baseball will open its doors to Negroes."[7]

At the end of that meeting, Rickey offered Robinson a $3,500 bonus and a salary of $600 per month to play in 1946 for the Montreal Royals. They were the Dodgers' top farm team in the International League. If he did well, the next stop would be the major league Brooklyn Dodgers.

For the United States, 1945 was a year of change. World War II finally ended with the defeat of both Germany and Japan. President Franklin Roosevelt died in April and was replaced by Harry S. Truman. And in Brooklyn, a revolution had begun.

Jackie Robinson and Branch Rickey. Each needed the other to be strong to break through baseball's color line.

Close to First

Jackie Robinson was not the first African-American to wear a Dodger uniform. On April 6, 1945, black players Terris McDuffie and Dave "Showboat" Thomas showed up for a tryout at the Brooklyn Dodgers' spring training camp at Bear Mountain, New York. A recent New York law forbade job discrimination based upon race. The two hoped that that law would enable them to play organized baseball. However, neither displayed enough skill to make the team.

Terris McDuffie

Catcher Roy Campanella was almost signed instead of Robinson. He had talked to Rickey a week before Robinson, but thought that Rickey wanted him for a new black team and was not interested. When he heard that Robinson had signed, Campanella was worried. Had he missed his chance to play in the majors?

Luckily, he did not. Rickey eventually signed him, and Campanella became one of the best catchers in baseball. He won three National League Most Valuable Player awards.

Roy Campanella

Robinson's signing was kept secret from the press and the public until October 23, 1945. On that day, officials of the Montreal Royals promised a big announcement. Some thought Babe Ruth was going to be named manager. Instead they told the world that Jackie Robinson would play for them in 1946.

Reactions came quickly. Some thought that Robinson was the wrong player to be plucked from the Negro Leagues. Star pitcher Bob Feller predicted that Robinson wouldn't be able to hit because he had too much upper-body muscle. "If he were a white man I doubt they would even consider him as big league material," he said.[1]

Jimmy Powers, a columnist for New York's *Daily News*, called Robinson a 1,000-to-1 shot to make it. Now with the war over, he said, the flood of talented returning ballplayers would overwhelm Robinson.

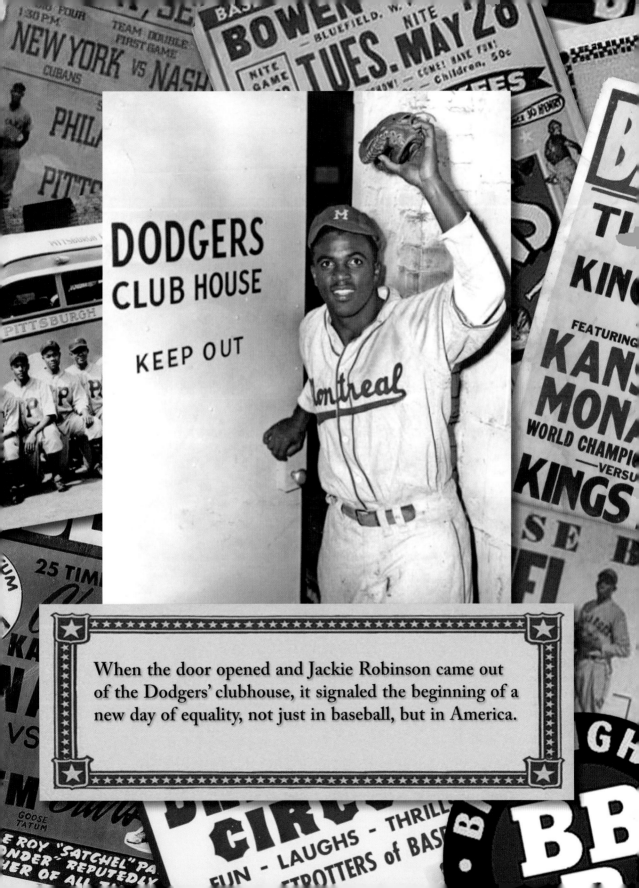

When the door opened and Jackie Robinson came out of the Dodgers' clubhouse, it signaled the beginning of a new day of equality, not just in baseball, but in America.

The Sporting News thought that the competition in the International League was too tough.

Some ballplayers were outraged. They did not want to play on the same field as an African-American. One said that many ballplayers from the South found it extremely distasteful to be asked to play with Robinson. Others claimed that signing a black player was okay by them. They just didn't want to play with or against him.

Robinson's trials began in spring training in Florida in 1946. He and his new bride Rachael were staying with a black family in Sanford, Florida. One night they got a call. A group was planning a march to the house. They were going to burn a cross on the lawn. Rickey was afraid there would be violence.[2] The Robinsons had to flee.

Jackie and Rachel Robinson overcame incredible pressures. Rachel earned a nursing degree before marrying Jackie. She later became an assistant professor at Yale University.

Robinson training with Montreal as Branch Rickey watches.

Robinson got off to a slow start in spring training with the Royals. Once again people said that he wasn't good enough. Some local laws forbade blacks and whites from playing baseball together. Officials told Robinson he could be arrested if he played. All this weighed on his mind. It affected his performance on the field.

Somehow Robinson fought through these troubles. He played well enough to make the Montreal team. On April 18, the Royals opened the season against the Jersey City Giants in Jersey City, New Jersey.

Jackie crosses the plate April 18, 1946, with his first home run in the minor leagues.

Robinson went four-for-five in that game. He also hit a home run. On the base paths he was always moving. He took long leads, pretended to steal, and danced around. He upset the opposing pitcher so much that the pitcher balked home a run for Montreal.

The Robinsons shared a home with a kind Montreal woman. Jackie and Rachel were expecting a baby soon. Jackie relaxed. The Montreal crowd loved him. He ignored the many times other players deliberately spiked him. Opposing pitchers would throw at his head to try to injure him. He shook it off and roared through the season. He hit .349 with 40 stolen bases. He won the league's batting championship, the first Royal ever to do so. Robinson was named the league's Most Valuable Player.

In the International League World Series Robinson led the Royals to victory. After the final game win in Montreal, happy fans carried him around the park on their shoulders. They didn't want to let him go. He was their hero.

It was now obvious that Robinson was skilled enough. Yet something else happened too. His class and determination convinced many people to embrace racial equality. One was his manager. He had begun the season wondering if a black person was a human being. He

ended it by shaking Robinson's hand and praising him. In the 1940s, when a white man shook a black man's hand, it meant that they were equals.

Now Jackie just had to do it all over again—in Brooklyn.

In early 1947 Robinson joined the Brooklyn Dodgers for spring training. Some Dodgers started a petition. It said that they would rather be traded than play on a team with a black man.

Fiery Dodger manager Leo Durocher learned of the petition. He called a team meeting at one o'clock in the morning in an empty kitchen at the team's training facility. The sleepy players arrived in pajamas and underwear. Durocher yelled at them. He told them their petition was worthless.

"I'd play an elephant if he could win for me and this fellow Robinson is no elephant," Durocher said. "This fellow is a great player. He's gonna win pennants. He's gonna put money in your pocket and mine."[3]

Then he said something that showed how well he understood the future. "He's only the first, boys, only the first. Unless you wake up, these colored ballplayers are gonna run you right out of the park."[4]

Leo Durocher and Jackie Robinson

The petition died, and Robinson started the season with the Dodgers. The other team members were unsure of how to treat him. In late April, Brooklyn played the

Philadelphia Phillies. The Phillies screamed racial insults at Robinson. Their manager, Ben Chapman, was loudest of all.

The insults almost got to Robinson. He tried to ignore them as he had promised he would. The rest of the Dodgers knew that he could not react. They were furious. Finally infielder Eddie Stanky screamed at the Phillies: "You yellow-bellied cowards! Why don't you yell at somebody who can answer back?"[5]

The Phillies meant to upset Robinson. Their insults, however, had the opposite effect. The Dodgers united behind their teammate. As Rickey recalled, "Chapman made Jackie a real member of the Dodgers."[6]

Robinson was the same exciting player for the Dodgers as he had been for the Royals. He hit .297 with 12 home runs and 48 runs batted in. On the bases he was a bundle of energy. He repeatedly made opposing pitchers make mistakes. He was named the National League's Rookie of the Year. He did all this despite the negative treatment he received.

The Dodgers won the 1947 National League pennant. Robinson was a big reason for that. He had proven that color did not matter.

John Jorgensen, Pee Wee Reese, Eddie Stanky, and Jackie Robinson of the Brooklyn Dodgers.

Spotlight Heroes:
Neil Churchill and Monte Irvin

The Bismarck Churchills in 1935. Satchel Paige is center in back row, Neil Churchill is kneeling in the center.

Neil Churchill was a pioneer for baseball integration. He owned a car dealership in Bismarck, North Dakota. A semi-pro player with Bismarck's baseball team, he bought the team in 1933. He decided the best way to improve his team was to sign talented black players. Among them were Satchel Paige, Hilton Smith, and Ted "Double Duty" Radcliffe. The club won the National Baseball Conference semi-pro championship in 1935.

In the early 1940s, Monte Irvin was one of the best outfielders in the Negro Leagues. He was young and fast, a good hitter and fielder. He spent 1943–1945 in the military. After he left the service, Branch Rickey asked him to play for him. Rickey did not make it clear that he was seeking a player to integrate baseball. Irvin turned him down and returned to the Negro Leagues. In 1949, Irvin joined the New York Giants and became a star. In 1973 he was elected to the baseball Hall of Fame.

Monte Irvin

Larry Doby never received the attention Robinson did. However, as the second black player to sign in the majors, he faced many of the same trials as Robinson.

Doby was born in Camden, South Carolina, on December 13, 1923. He moved to Paterson, New Jersey, and became one of the state's most famous high school athletes. He played basketball, football, track, and baseball. In May 1942, Doby began playing second base for the Negro Leagues' Newark Eagles. This was even before he had graduated high school. He quickly became one of the team's stars.

Doby was drafted in 1943 and stayed in the military until January 1946. That spring he rejoined the Eagles and hit .348. His great play helped the Eagles win the Negro American League pennant. In

Larry Doby was the second black baseball player in major league baseball. He was the first in the American League. He signed with the Cleveland Indians in 1947.

Effa Manley owned and ran the Newark Eagles with her husband Abe. She also served as the treasurer of the Negro Leagues. Manley was the first woman elected to Baseball's Hall of Fame, inducted in 2006.

the Negro League World Series, the Eagles faced the mighty Kansas City Monarchs. Doby helped the Eagles beat the Monarchs in seven games. He was one of the brightest young stars of Negro League baseball.

As the 1947 baseball season opened, Doby continued his excellent play. The Eagles' season was divided into two parts. Doby hit a red-hot .458 with 14 home runs in the first half. Bill Veeck owned the Cleveland Indians in baseball's American League. He had been looking for a good young black ballplayer. The Indians were a top team. They needed one or two more good players to help them win the pennant. Veeck knew that Doby could help them.

On July 1, 1947, Veeck called Eagles executive Effa Manley. He offered her $10,000 for Doby.

"I know very well that if he was a white boy and a free agent you'd give him a hundred thousand," Manley said. She knew that Veeck could sign Doby and not give the Eagles anything. This is what Rickey had done. The Monarchs had received nothing for Robinson. "But if you feel you're being fair offering me ten, I guess I'll have to take it," she said.[1]

On July 5, 1947, Veeck signed Doby to a contract. He would be the first black player in the American League, and it was big news. "Just

remember that they play with a little white ball and a stick of wood up here just like they did in your league," Veeck told a nervous Doby.[2]

Doby then put on his uniform and got ready to play. Unlike Robinson, he was not going to the minor leagues first. He had no time to find out how people—including his teammates—would react to him.

Years later, after he had had time to think about it, Doby didn't regret stepping straight into the majors. "I look at myself as more fortunate than Jack [Robinson]," he said. "If I had gone through hell in the minors, then I'd have to go through it again in the majors. Once was enough!"[3]

Cleveland erupted over Doby's signing. People debated the "correctness" of signing a black ballplayer. Veeck received about 20,000 angry letters from upset people. He answered many of those letters himself.

Doby got off to a slow start with Cleveland. In 1947 he played in just 29 games and hit .156.

In his second year Doby showed his talent. He hit .301 with 14 home runs.

Doby never said much. Veeck had asked him not to say anything. Once, however, in Washington, D.C., his true feelings slipped out. "I don't want to be a symbol—I just want to be a big league player," he said.[4]

In 1947, Indians Manager Lou Boudreau used Doby mainly as a pinch-hitter. He hit just .156. The Indians fell out of the pennant race. This got critics started again. They said Doby was signed just for show. "If Doby were white," said future Hall of Famer Rogers Hornsby, "he wouldn't be considered good enough to play semi-pro."[5]

Doby felt uneasy. What if he wasn't good enough to play in the majors? Then the Indians added to his doubts. They asked him to learn how to play the outfield in the off-season. Doby's natural position was second base. Doby was filled with uncertainty about his future. When he reported to the Indians' spring training in Tuscon, Arizona, he was

told that he couldn't stay at the hotel with the rest of his teammates. Doby was confused, frightened, and alone.

Then something amazing happened. Doby began to excel. At bat he hit .358. In the field, he worked tirelessly with legendary outfielder Tris Speaker. He became a good outfielder. By the end of the spring, the scared, timid boy of 1947 was gone. In his place was one of the Indians' top outfielders.

Doby became one of the best hitters in the American League. In both 1952 and 1954 he hit 32 home runs and drove home over 100 runs.

In 2001 Doby was named one of the 100 greatest players in the history of the Cleveland Indians.

In 1948 Doby was a different player. He hit .301 with 14 home runs. He helped the Indians win the American League pennant. His stellar play continued in the 1948 World Series against the Boston Braves. He hit .318 and won Game Four with a home run. The Indians beat the Braves in six games and became world champs.

Doby and Robinson had proved that a player could be great no matter his (or her) race. There was no place for discrimination in baseball. Thanks to them and Branch Rickey, the door was now open for other black players to join the major leagues.

Ford Frick and Happy Chandler

Ford Frick

In May 1947, during Jackie Robinson's first season, some members of the St. Louis Cardinals threatened to strike. National League President Ford Frick learned of the protest. He said he would suspend anyone who struck even if it damaged the league for years. "This is the United States of America and one citizen has as much right to play as another," he said.[6] The strike collapsed.

Some feel that the door for black players opened when baseball commissioner Kenesaw Mountain Landis died on November 25, 1944. In April 1945, baseball owners chose A.B. "Happy" Chandler as Landis' successor. The new commissioner fully supported Branch Rickey's plans.

Happy Chandler (right) joined forces with Branch Rickey and chose to approve Jackie Robinson's contract, but he faced the consequences later as the owners did not renew his contract after only one term. He later became Governor of Kentucky for the second time. While commissioner, Chandler created the first pension fund for Major Leaguers.

AN END

Americans were used to being segregated in public places. There were separate bathrooms and water fountains for black people and white people. They had separate seating areas on buses—whites in front, blacks in back. Would black and white fans sit together in baseball stands?

"[White fans] don't want to sit with Negroes and they'll stop coming to our games. . . . To bring in Negroes is to court financial ruin,"[1] said New York Yankees General Manager George Weiss.

But Robinson broke the color barrier there, too. Fans came from all over to see him play. At one Dodgers-Reds game in Cincinnati, African-American fans from as far away as Mobile, Alabama, came to the game—a 700-mile trip.

For many decades, American society operated according to the unjust idea of "separate but equal." This meant that there were separate rules and facilities—such as the water fountain above—for white people and black people.

Dave Hoskins and manager Dutch Meyer of the Dallas Eagles

"Jackie's nimble, Jackie's quick, Jackie's making the turnstiles click,"[2] wrote sportswriter Wendell Smith.

The same was true with Doby. On July 14, 1948, in Cleveland, 26,000 African-Americans and 64,877 fans total came out to see a game between the Dodgers and Doby's Cleveland Indians. One out of every six black citizens of Cleveland attended the game.[3]

Black players also affected minor league attendance. Pitcher Dave Hoskins was called the "savior of the Texas League" because he drew big crowds whenever he pitched. Slugging first baseman Luke Easter was very popular in the Pacific Coast League. Thousands of people showed up early at games just to see him take batting practice.

Black ballplayers added fans and made money for white baseball. The opposite was true for black baseball.

At first black club owners thought that the success of black ballplayers would mean more money for them

LUKE EASTER
first base CLEVELAND INDIANS

Luke Easter card

too. However, black baseball fans began following Robinson and the Dodgers. They ignored Negro League teams, and attendance dropped. It got worse as 1947 went on. By August, just 2,000 fans were coming to see the Negro League champion Newark Eagles. The Eagles' total attendance sank like a stone. In 1946 it was over 120,000. In 1947 it was just 57,000. The Eagles lost $22,000 in 1947.[4] Almost every Negro League team lost money that year.

Women began playing in the Negro Leagues. Toni Stone played second base for the Indianapolis Clowns and hit .243

By the next year, top Negro League teams drew just 1,200 fans per game. Some crowds numbered just 700.

"We couldn't even draw flies," remembered Negro League first baseman Buck Leonard.[5]

By 1948 there were over a dozen black players in the major leagues. Satchel Paige had been the biggest drawing card in black baseball. Then he joined the Cleveland Indians. The Eagles attracted just 35,000 fans for the entire 1948 season. At the end of the season they disbanded. The Homestead Grays and New York Black Yankees did the same. The Negro National League folded. Its remaining teams joined the Negro American League.

By 1950, five big league teams had been integrated: Dodgers, Giants, Indians, Braves, and Browns. Three years later it was seven teams. Negro League clubs could not attract enough fans to make

1948 champion Birmingham Black Barons' Rickwood Field Entrance during it's heyday. Once African-Americans began playing professional baseball, fans followed those teams instead of Negro League teams.

money. To raise cash, they sold their best players to the major leagues. The fans followed.

Negro teams tried other ways to raise money. They cut player salaries to $200 per month. They played games in small towns where people did not often see professional baseball. They hired clowns and other entertainers to perform before games.

Nothing helped. By 1957 there were 36 African-Americans on major league teams. This included some of the brightest stars in the game: Ernie Banks (Chicago Cubs), Willie Mays (New York Giants), and Frank Robinson (Cincinnati Reds). In 1959, Elijah "Pumpsie" Green joined the Boston Red Sox. All 16 major league teams now had black players.

A new decade of optimism and promise started in the United States in 1960. Fair-minded John F. Kennedy was the new president. Martin Luther King was leading a civil rights movement. This gave blacks hope that equal rights would finally be theirs.

Meanwhile, just four Negro League teams remained: the Kansas City Monarchs, Detroit-New Orleans Stars, Birmingham Black Barons, and the Raleigh (North Carolina) Tigers. At the end of 1960, the Negro American League folded. A few other teams continued barnstorming—traveling from place to place and playing wherever they thought they could draw fans. Eventually, they all vanished.

In 1971, Satchel Paige became a member of the Baseball Hall of Fame in Cooperstown, New York. The next few years saw other Negro League greats become members as well. The skill of Negro League players was finally being recognized.

Today there are books and movies about Negro League baseball and its players. Club names are on T-shirts. There is even a Negro Leagues museum in Kansas City, Missouri.

The Negro Leagues may be gone, but they will not be forgotten.

A museum dedicated to the Negro Leagues opened in 1997 in Kansas City, Missouri. It shares the complex with the American Jazz Museum and helps ensure that interest in black baseball will never vanish.

Frank Robinson: Manager

Frank Robinson

In late 1974 the Cleveland Indians made history again. They named Frank Robinson the first African-American player-manager. Robinson had a great career as an outfielder. He had played with the Cincinnati Reds, Baltimore Orioles, and several other teams. As manager for the Indians, he was still on the roster. For his first at-bat on April 8, 1975, Robinson hit a home run.

Frank Robinson paved the way for many African-American managers, including Dusty Baker (right), Lloyd McClendon, Don Baylor, Willie Randolph, Cecil Cooper.

Dusty Baker

Barrier Breakers

The First African-American Players for Each Team

Team	Player	Debut Date
Boston Braves	Sam Jethroe	April 18, 1950
Boston Red Sox	Pumpsie Green	July 21, 1959
Brooklyn Dodgers	*Jackie Robinson	April 15, 1947
Chicago Cubs	*Ernie Banks	September 17, 1953
Chicago White Sox	Minnie Minoso	May 1, 1951
Cleveland Indians	*Larry Doby	July 5, 1947
Cincinnati Reds	Nino Escalera	April 17, 1954
	Chuck Harmon	April 17, 1954
Detroit Tigers	Ossie Virgil Sr.	June 6, 1958
New York Giants	*Monte Irvin	July 8, 1949
	Hank Thompson	July 8, 1949
New York Yankees	Elston Howard	April 14, 1955
Philadelphia Athletics	Bob Trice	September 13, 1953
Philadelphia Phillies	John Kennedy	April 22, 1957
Pittsburgh Pirates	Curt Roberts	April 13, 1954
St. Louis Browns	Hank Thompson	July 17, 1947
St. Louis Cardinals	Tom Alston	April 13, 1954
Washington Senators	Carlos Paula	September 6, 1954

*Member of Baseball Hall of Fame

Chapter One

1. Robert Paterson, *Only the Ball Was White* (New York: Oxford University Press, 1970), p. 16.

2. Geoffrey C. Ward and Ken Burns, *Baseball* (New York: Alfred A. Knopf, 1994), p. 41.

3. Lawrence D. Hogan, *Shades of Glory* (Washington, D.C.: National Geographic Society, 2006), p. 55.

Chapter Two

1. Roger Kahn, *Rickey & Robinson* (New York: Rodale, 2014), p. ix.

2. Ibid., p. x.

3. William C. Kashatus, *Jackie & Campy* (Lincoln: University of Nebraska Press, 2014) p. 34.

4. Kahn, p. 25.

5. Ibid., p. 40.

6. Kashatus, p. 51.

7. Kahn, p. 107.

Chapter Three

1. Arnold Rampersad, *Jackie Robinson* (New York: Alfred A. Knopf, 1997), p. 130.

2. Roger Kahn, *Rickey & Robinson* (New York: Rodale, 2014), p. 200.

3. Kahn, p. 118.

4. Ibid., p. 118.

5. Rampersad, p. 173.

6. Ibid.

Chapter Four

1. Paul Dickson, *Bill Veeck* (New York: Walker & Company, 2012), p. 126.

2. Joseph Thomas Moore, *Pride Against Prejudice* (New York: Praeger, 1988), p. 46.

3. Ibid., p. 47.

4. Dickson, p. 131.

5. Ibid., p. 133.

6. Robert Paterson, *Only the Ball Was White* (New York: Oxford University Press, 1970), p. 199.

Chapter Five

1. Roger Kahn, *Rickey & Robinson* (New York: Rodale, 2014), p. 22.

2. Ibid., p. 44.

3. Larry Moffi and Jonathan Kronstadt, *Crossing the Line* (Jefferson, North Carolina: McFarland & Company, 1994), p. 8.

4. James Overmyer, *Effa Manley and the Newark Eagles* (Metuchen, New Jersey: The Scarecrow Press, Inc., 1993), p. 236.

5. Arnold Rampersad, *Jackie Robinson* (New York: Alfred A. Knopf, 1997), p. 132.

Works Consulted

Dickson, Paul. *Bill Veeck*. New York: Walker & Company, 2012.

Dunkel, Tom. *Color Blind*. New York: Atlantic Monthly Press, 2013.

Hogan, Lawrence D. *Shades of Glory*. Washington, D.C.: National Geographic Society, 2006.

Holway, John. *The Complete Book of Baseball's Negro Leagues: The Other Half of Baseball History*. Fern Park, Florida: Hastings House Publishers, 2001.

Kahn, Roger. *Rickey & Robinson*. New York: Rodale, 2014.

Kashatus, William C. *Jackie & Campy*. Lincoln: University of Nebraska Press, 2014.

Moffi, Larry, and Jonathan Kronstadt. *Crossing the Line*. Jefferson, North Carolina: McFarland & Company, 1994.

Moore, Joseph Thomas. *Pride Against Prejudice*. New York: Praeger, 1988.

The Negro Leagues Book, edited by Dick Clark and Larry Lester. Cleveland: The Society for American Baseball Research, 1994.

Overmyer, James. *Effa Manley and the Newark Eagles*. Metuchen, New Jersey: The Scarecrow Press, Inc., 1993.

Peterson, Robert. *Only the Ball was White*. New York: Oxford University Press, 1970.

Pietrusza, David. *Judge and Jury*. South Bend, Indiana: Diamond Communications, Inc., 1998.

Rampersad, Arnold. *Jackie Robinson*. New York: Alfred A. Knopf, 1997.

Veeck, Bill, and Ed Linn. *Veeck—As in Wreck*. New York: G.P. Putnam's Sons, 1962.

Ward, Geoffrey C., and Ken Burns. *Baseball*. New York: Alfred A. Knopf, 1994.

Books

Jacobs, Greg. *The Everything Kids' Baseball Book: From Baseball's History to Today's Favorite Players—With Lots of Home Run Fun In Between!* Fort Collins, Colorado: Adams Media, 2014.

Meltzer, Brad. *I Am Jackie Robinson (Ordinary People Change the World)*. New York: Dial Books, 2015.

Myers, Walter Dean. *Down to the Last Out, the Journal of Biddy Owens, the Negro Leagues*. New York: Scholastic Paperbacks, 2013.

Robinson, Sharon. *Jackie Robinson, American Hero*. New York: Scholastic Paperbacks, 2013.

Tooke, Wes. *King of the Mound: My Summer with Satchel Paige*. New York: Simon and Schuster Books for Young Readers, 2012.

On the Internet

Baseball Hall of Fame for Kids
    http://baseballhall.org/visit/sandlot-kids
Jackie Robinson Biography
    http://www.ducksters.com/sports/jackie_robinson.php
Larry Doby Biography
    http://baseballhall.org/hof/doby-larry
Negro League Baseball
    http://www.negroleaguebaseball.com/
Negro League Baseball Museum
    https://www.nlbm.com/

balk (BAWK)—To start a pitch but not release the ball; when a pitcher balks, the runners are allowed to advance one base.

barnstorm (BARN-storm)—To tour an area putting on performances.

bigotry (BIG-uh-tree)—Hating or refusing to accept the members of a particular group.

court-martial (KORT-mar-shul)—To charge someone of a crime in a military court.

discriminate (dis-KRIH-mih-nayt)—To treat someone unfairly based on racist beliefs.

executive (ek-ZEK-yoo-tiv)—A person who is in charge of running an organization.

forfeit (FOR-fit)—To lose a game by agreement instead of through play.

International League (in-ter-NASH-uh-nul LEEG)—A minor-league baseball league formed when teams from the Eastern League, the New York State League, and the Ontario (Canada) League were combined.

lynch (LINCH)—To put someone to death without legal authority.

racism (RAY-sism)—A belief that people who look or act like oneself are better than others, and that it is okay to be mean to those others.

segregate (SEH-grih-gayt)—To separate groups based on race, gender, or religion.

successor (suk-SES-or)—Someone or something that comes after.

PHOTO CREDITS: Pp.l, 3, 13, 33, 35—loc.gov; p. 14—Toney Fischer; p. 39—Mark Goebel; p. 40—Jerry Reuss; All other photos—Public Domain. Every measure has been taken to find all copyright holders of material used in this book. In the event any mistakes or omissions have happened within, attempts to correct them will be made in future editions of the book.

INDEX